M000118606

itty**bitty**books™

BIBLE PROMISES

FOR THE

GRADUATE

THOMAS NELSON PUBLISHERS
Nashville

Published in Nashville, Tennessee by Thomas
Nelson, Publishers and distributed in Canada
by Lawson Falle, Ltd., Cambridge, Ontario.

**Library of Congress
Cataloging-in-Publication Data**

Bible promises for graduates.
      p.   cm. — (An Itty Bitty book)
      ISBN 0-8407-6893-1
      1. God—Promises. 2. High school
graduates—Prayer-books and devotions—
English. I. Series.
BT180.P7B53 1993
242'.63—dc20   92-41940
                            CIP

Printed in Hong Kong.
1 2 3 4 5 6 7 — 98 97 96 95 94 93

TABLE OF CONTENTS

You are about to embark on a grand adventure. Life is full of hope and promises, but there may also be disappointment and tremendous challenges ahead as well. The Bible has always been a guide to help Christians deal with sin and confusion, and it continues to be a light by which to walk through the occasional darkness of this world.

I hope these passages from the Bible will help you in the coming years. Use them as devotionals, or just as signposts to tell you which way to turn. Just remember: you are never alone. God is always with you.

"Your word is a lamp to my feet and a light to my path."

Psalm 119:105

Spiritual Growth

All Scripture is given by inspiration of God, and is profitable for doctrine, for reproof, for correction, for instruction in righteousness. That the man of God may be complete, thoroughly equipped for every good work.

2 TIMOTHY 3:16–17

Let all the earth fear the Lord; let all the inhabitants of the world stand in awe of Him. For He spoke, and it was done; He commanded, and it stood fast.

PSALM 33:8–9

3

For whatever things were written before were written for our learning, that we through the patience and comfort of the Scriptures might have hope.   ROMANS 15:4

So then faith comes by hearing, and hearing by the word of God.   ROMANS 10:17

For the Scripture says, "Whoever believes on Him will not be put to shame."
ROMANS 10:11

And now, brethern, I commend you to God and to the word of His grace, which is able to build you up and give you an inheritance among all those who are sanctified." ACTS 20:32

The works of His
hands are verity and
justice; all His precepts
are sure. They stand
fast forever and ever,
and are done in truth
and uprightness.

PSALM 11:7–8

Therefore the law was our tutor to bring us to Christ, that we might be justified by faith.   GALATIANS 3:24

For as the body without the spirit is dead, so faith without works is dead also.
JAMES 2:26

8

*S*tand therefore,
having girded your
waist with truth,
having put on the
breastplate of
righteousness.

EPHESIANS 6:14

Let no one deceive you with empty words, for because of these things the wrath of God comes upon the sons of disobedience.

EPHESIANS 5:6

For God has not given us a spirit of fear, but of power and of love and of a sound mind.   2 TIMOTHY 1:7

Be of good courage, and He shall strengthen your heart, all you who hope in the Lord.
PSALM 31:24

For in that He Himself has suffered, being tempted, He is able to aid those who are tempted.

HEBREWS 2:18

Listen, my beloved brethren: Has God not chosen the poor of this world to be rich in faith and heirs of the kingdom which He promised to those who love Him?

JAMES 2:5

But without faith it is impossible to please Him, for he who comes to God must believe that He is, and that He is a rewarder of those who diligently seek Him.

HEBREWS 11:6

For in it the righteousness of God is revealed from faith to faith; as it is written, "The just shall live by faith." ROMANS 1:17

Now faith is the substance of things hoped for, the evidence of things not seen. HEBREWS 11:1

Now may the God of hope fill you with all joy and peace in believing, that you may abound in hope by the power of the Holy Spirit.

ROMANS 15:13

Then Jesus spoke to them again, saying, "I am the light of the world. He who follows Me shall not walk in darkness, but have the light of life."

JOHN 8:12

17

The fear of the Lord is the beginning of wisdom; a good understanding have all those who do His commandments. His praise endures forever.

PSALM 111:10

18

But go and learn what this means: 'I desire mercy and not sacrifice.' For I did not come to call the righteous, but sinners, to repentance."

MATTHEW 9:13

F or it is the God who commanded light to shine out of darkness who has shone in our hearts to give the light of the knowledge of the glory of God in the face of Jesus Christ.

2 CORINTHIANS 4:6

20

Yet in all these things we are more than conquerors through Him who loved us.   ROMANS 8:37

Evil men do not understand justice, but those who seek the Lord understand all.
PROVERBS 28:5

But thanks be to God, *who gives us the victory through our Lord Jesus Christ.*

1 CORINTHIANS 15:57

Blessed are the pure in heart, *for they shall see God.*

MATTHEW 5:8

Personal Needs

Trust in the Lord with all your heart, and lean not on your own understanding; in all your ways acknowledge Him, and He shall direct your paths. PROVERBS 3:5–6

Υour ears shall hear a word behind you, saying, "This is the way, walk in it," whenever you turn to the right hand or whenever you turn to the left. ISAIAH 30:21

But those who wait on the Lord shall renew their strength; they shall mount up with wings like eagles, they shall run and not be weary, they shall walk and not faint.

ISAIAH 40:31

God is our refuge
and strength, a very
present help in trouble.
PSALM 46:1

Now may the
Lord of peace Himself
give you peace always
in every way. The Lord
be with you all.
2 THESSALONIANS 3:16

If any of you lacks wisdom, let him ask of God, who gives to all liberally and without reproach, and it will be given to him.

JAMES 1:5

Therefore submit to God. Resist the devil and he will flee from you.   JAMES 4:7

A man's heart plans his way, but the Lord directs his steps.
PROVERBS 16:9

For I will give you a mouth and wisdom which all your adversaries will not be able to contradict or resist." LUKE 21:15

I can do all things through Christ who strengthens me.

PHILIPPIANS 4:13

Therefore, brethren, be even more diligent to make your calling and election sure, for if you do these things you will never stumble.

2 PETER 1:10

Ask, and it will be given to you; seek, and you will find; knock and it will be opened to you. For everyone who asks receives, and he who seeks finds, and to him who knocks it will be opened."

MATTHEW 7:7–8

So we may boldly say: "The Lord is my helper: I will not fear. What can man do to me?"   HEBREWS 13:6

And whatever you ask in My name, that I will do, that the Father may be glorified in the Son."
JOHN 14:13

And whatever we ask we receive from Him, because we keep His commandments and do those things that are pleasing in His sight. 1 JOHN 3:22

"**A**nd all things, whatever you ask in prayer, believing, you will receive."
MATTHEW 21:22

But know that the Lord has set apart for Himself him who is godly; the Lord will hear when I call to Him.   PSALM 4:3

Call to Me, and I will answer you, and show you great and mighty things, which you do not know."
JEREMIAH 33:3

Because Your lovingkindness is better than life, my lips shall praise You. PSALM 63:3

For we are His workmanship, created in Christ Jesus for good works, which God prepared beforehand that we should walk in them.

EPHESIANS 2:10

The Lord is good, a stronghold in the day of trouble; and He knows those who trust in Him.   NAHUM 1:7

The Lord is my shepherd; I shall not want.   PSALM 23:1

Let us therefore come boldly to the throne of grace, that we may obtain mercy and find grace to help in time of need.

HEBREWS 4:16

Blessed is the man who endures temptation; for when he has been proved, he will receive the crown of life which the Lord has promised to those who love Him.

JAMES 1:12

Therefore I say to you, *whatever things you ask when you pray, believe that you receive them, and you will have them."*

MARK 11:24

But these are written that you may believe that Jesus is the Christ, the Son of God, and that believing you may have life in His name.

JOHN 20:31

For He satisfies the longing soul, and fills the hungry soul with goodness.

PSALM 107:9

But seek first the kingdom of God and His righteousness, and all these things shall be added to you."

MATTHEW 6:33

I *will call upon the Lord, who is worthy to be praised; so shall I be saved from my enemies.*

PSALM 18:3

Relationships

For whoever does
the will of My Father
in heaven is My
brother and sister and
mother."

MATTHEW 12:50

I will be a Father to you, and you shall be My sons and daughters, says the Lord Almighty."

2 CORINTHIANS 6:18

By this all will know that you are My disciples, if you have love for one another."

JOHN 13:35

But I say to you,
love your enemies,
bless those who curse
you, do good to those
who hate you, and
pray for those who
spitefully use you and
persecute you."

MATTHEW 5:44

For if you forgive men their trespasses, your heavenly Father will also forgive you. But if you do not forgive men their trespasses, neither will your Father forgive your trespasses."

MATTHEW 6:14–15

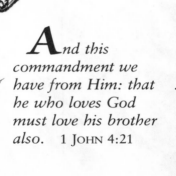

*A*nd this commandment we have from Him: that he who loves God must love his brother also.   1 JOHN 4:21

50

But do not forget to do good and to share, for with such sacrifices God is well pleased.

HEBREWS 13:16

Be of good
comfort, be of one
mind, live in peace;
and the God of love
and peace will be with
you.

2 CORINTHIANS 13:11

*A*nd *whenever
you stand praying, if
you have anything
against anyone, forgive
him, that your Father
in heaven may also
forgive you your
trespasses.*

MARK 11:25

But whoever has this world's goods, and sees his brother in need, and shuts up his heart from him, how does the love of God abide in him?

1 JOHN 3:17

54

With the pure
You will show Yourself
pure; and with the
devious You will show
Yourself shrewd.

PSALM 18:26

And who is he
who will harm you if
you become followers
of what is good?

1 PETER 3:13

Give, and it will be given to you; good measure, pressed down, shaken together, and running over will be put into your bosom. For with the same measure that you use, it will be measured back to you.

LUKE 6:38

Two are better than one, because they have a good reward for their labor. For if they fall, one will lift up his companion. But woe to him who is alone when he falls, for he has no one to help him up.

ECCLESIASTES 4:9–10

For God is not unjust to forget your work and labor of love which you have shown toward His name, in that you have ministered to the saints, and do minister.

HEBREWS 6:10

May the God of patience and comfort grant you to be like-minded toward one another, according to Christ Jesus.

ROMANS 15:5

Let your light so shine before men, that they may see your good works and glorify your Father in heaven. MATTHEW 5:16

*A*nd whatever
you do, do it heartily,
as to the Lord and not
to men, knowing that
from the Lord you will
receive the reward of
the inheritance; for
you serve the Lord
Christ.

COLOSSIANS 3:23–24

Those who are wise shall shine like the brightness of the firmament, and those who turn many to righteousness like the stars forever and ever.

DANIEL 12:3

Again I say to you that if two of you agree on earth concerning anything that they ask, it will be done for them by My Father in heaven. For where two or three are gathered together in My name, I am there in the midst of them."

MATTHEW 18:19–20

Now we exhort you, brethren, warn those who are unruly, comfort the fainthearted, uphold the weak, be patient with all.

1 THESSALONIANS 5:14

For whatever is born of God overcomes the world. And this is the victory that has overcome the world—our faith. Who is he who overcomes the world, but he who believes that Jesus is the Son of God?

1 JOHN 5:4–5

You did not choose Me, but I chose you and appointed you that you should go and bear fruit, and that your fruit should remain, that whatever you ask the Father in My name He may give you. JOHN 15:16

66

Salvation
and
Eternal
Life

And if I go and prepare a place for you, I will come again and receive you to Myself; that where I am, there you may be also." JOHN 14:3

The Lord is not
slack concerning His
promise, as some
count slackness, but is
longsuffering toward
us, not willing that any
should perish but that
all should come to
repentance.

2 PETER 3:9

For God did not
send His Son into the
world to condemn the
world, but that the
world through Him
might be saved."

JOHN 3:17

For the Son of Man has come to seek and to save that which was lost." LUKE 19:10

Jesus said to her, "I am the resurrection and the life. He who believes in Me, though he may die, he shall live." JOHN 11:25

For I delivered to
you first of all that
which I also received;
that Christ died for
our sins according to
the Scriptures.

1 CORINTHIANS 15:3

But God demonstrates His own love toward us, in that while we were still sinners, Christ died for us.   ROMANS 5:8

For you are all sons of God through faith in Christ Jesus.
GALATIANS 3:26

For the Lord God is a sun and shield; the Lord will give grace and glory; no good thing will He withhold from those who walk uprightly. PSALM 84:11

That they may walk in My statutes and keep My judgements and do them; and they shall be My people, and I will be their God."

EZEKIEL 11:20

But we believe
that through the grace
of the Lord Jesus
Christ we shall be
saved in the same
manner as they."

ACTS 15:11

He who overcomes shall be clothed in white garments, and I will not blot out his name from the Book of Life; but I will confess his name before My Father and before His angels."

REVELATION 3:5

For by grace you
have been saved
through faith, and that
not of yourselves; it is
the gift of God.

EPHESIANS 2:8

*F*or this is God,
our God forever and
ever; He will be our
guide even to death.

PSALM 48:14

*A*nd it shall come
to pass that whoever
calls on the name of
the Lord shall be
saved." ACTS 2:21

79

Most assuredly, I say to you, he who believes in Me, the works that I do he will do also; and greater works than these he will do, because I go to My Father."

JOHN 14:12

Or do you despise the riches of His goodness, forbearance, and longsuffering, not knowing that the goodness of God leads you to repentance?

ROMANS 2:4

For you were like sheep going astray, but have now returned to the Shepherd and Overseer of your souls.

1 PETER 2:25

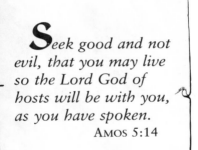

Seek good and not
evil, that you may live
so the Lord God of
hosts will be with you,
as you have spoken.

AMOS 5:14

Therefore whoever confesses Me before men, him I will also confess before My Father who is in heaven."

MATTHEW 10:32

Let us hold fast the confession of our hope without wavering, for He who promised is faithful.

HEBREWS 10:23

Yet I will rejoice in the Lord, I will joy in the God of my salvation.

HABAKKUK 3:18

But when the wicked turns from his wickedness and does what is lawful and right, he shall live because of it."

EZEKIEL 33:19

For God did not appoint us to wrath, but to obtain salvation through our Lord Jesus Christ, who died for us, that whether we wake or sleep, we should live together with Him.

1 THESSALONIANS 5:9–10

I, *even I, am He who blots out your transgressions for My own sake; and I will not remember your sins."* ISAIAH 43:25

88

He who believes in Him is not condemned, but he who does not believe is condemned already, because he has not believed in the name of the only begotten Son of God." JOHN 3:18